laudanum chapbook anthology:
volume one

Philip Terry
Stuart Mckenzie
Joey Connolly

series editor
Tiffany Anne Tondut

laudanum

Tiffany Anne Tondut is a London-based poet, editor and publisher. Her poetry has appeared in magazines, newspapers and anthologies including *Magma*, *The Rialto* and *Poetry News*.

First published in 2016 by laudanum
31 Rosedene, 77 Christchurch Ave
London NW6 7NU

Printed in England by Imprint Digital
Typesetting and book design by Tiffany Anne Tondut
Cover illustration © mystel / Shutterstock
Title page artwork © Liliya Shlapak / Shutterstock

Copyright © laudanum 2016

All rights reserved. No part of this publication may be reproduced, stored in a retrieval system or transmitted by any means without the prior permission in writing of the publisher, nor be otherwise circulated in any form of binding or cover other than that in which it is published and without a similar condition including this condition being imposed on the subsequent purchaser. Copyright remains with the authors.

Contents

Poet	**Chapbook**	**Page**
Philip Terry	*du Bellay*	5
Stuart McKenzie	*The Dead Weight of Beauty*	21
Joey Connolly	*Moderns*	33
Acknowledgements		48

Forward

For some years I've harboured a fondness for anthologies, twinned with a hopeless desire to anthologise (I hadn't the experience or means). What a happy privilege it is, then, to publish these three poets – Philip Terry, Joey Connolly and Stuart McKenzie – in this laudanum chapbook anthology, the first in a series of volumes binding poets of varying style and achievement.

Chapbooks are typically 10 poems (or pages) in length, and yet they offer the scope to experiment, a niche for shorter works or a means of introducing new talent. One of the advantages of combining chapbooks is the reader's chance of discovering poets by way of association – and to a more explorative level than single-poem anthologies.

Naturally, patterns and themes emerge. The chapbooks in this volume share the concept of reinvention. And where technique might differ, playfulness, vigour or perspective is communal (vice-versa). Communality is important – it allows for intertextuality; a process of movement.

Although quality can be a measure of success, this series isn't merely concerned with publishing 'the best', but to disseminate verse that is exciting and inspiring for poets and public alike. Every good poem has a job to do. Some are more accessible or challenging to read. These chapbook anthologies aim to deliver a more Taoist 'middle path' without the blandness of health & safety, just a healthy mix of sex and cerebrum, philosophy and play, poetry of the moment and the considered avant-garde.

Tiffany Anne Tondut
July 27, 2016
Cambridge / London

2

More learned men than I, Canton, will philosophise
With Macfarlane perched in the bole of a tree
And, so that the papers will fête them,
Dive naked into the waters of the Dart.
As for me, I don't give a toss about eco-poetry,
I'm not going to hug a tree to squeeze out a pentameter,
I leave that to next generation poets, nor will I make it all rhyme
By polishing my thought till it shines.
All I want, Canton, is to jot down
Blog sonnets or sonnet blogs
Without expecting to be made poet laureate.
And perhaps those who think themselves smart,
Imagining such things can be done by any old twat,
Will find, when they try to rip me off, the result is flat.

3

Before I was voted Head of Department,
At the worst possible moment in the
University's fifty year history,
I used to follow the steep path of Shakespeare and Dante,
Lifted up by the wings of poetry.
Now there's a sign reading FOOTPATH CLOSED,
And I have a stuffed in-tray to keep me busy,
So must tread a different road,
And learn to hold my tongue at Leadership Away-Days.
That's why, Schmidt, having missed the road that Maxwell
Followed to St. Lucia and back,
I am earwitness to the ordinary noise,
Lacking the strength and the puff to follow, like him,
The flight path that leads to Walcott's villa.

11

Even though nobody gives a fuck about poetry,
Even though it's no way to make a living wage,
Even though squaddies have no use for it,
And those who want to get on look at it with scorn.
Even though politicians think it's something to laugh at,
And the cleverest writers won't touch it with a barge pole,
Even though Terry is proof enough
Of the low esteem in which this craft is held.
Even though labour without profit seems idiotic to accountants,
Even though decorators won't accept a cheque from sound poets,
Even though dedication to the Muse is sure to make you skint,
Yet I'm not about to quit:
For writing alone eases my pain,
And the Muses have gifted me eight years writing and more.

12

Given all the business plans I have to write,
Given the invoices that pile up all day,
And given all the staff that bring me their complaints,
You are surprised that I find time for sonnets.
For literary theorists sonnets are little songs,
For me they are laments, and I sing them with tears,
And in doing so chase my torments away,
That is why, Munton, I still sing night and day.
So builders sing to fight off the boredom of their labour,
So dairy farmers when they sell their produce at a loss,
So backpackers who cannot get a flight back home,
So songwriters who have no luck with their girls,
So the fisherman chasing the diminishing shoal,
So the poor sod in prison who is doing time.

21

Butterfield, lord who refused to lord it over anyone,
Terry is dead. I'm like a
Tree lying across a road after a storm,
Exhibiting no more life than the odd green leaf.
If sometimes, like now, I still put pen to paper,
I write without feeling, just to give off steam,
Putting down the first words that come into my head –
I am pissed off and that's all too plain in my style.
Aspirational disciples of Andrew Motion,
Whose art holds a mirror up to nature,
Imitate the best lines of the Georgian poets.
I have no such lofty ambitions,
And next to such fine paintings my sketches
Are no more than a Banksy next to a Stanley Spencer.

32

I will become an expert in philately,
In pottery and chemistry too,
I will become a gifted linguist and – why not? –
Learn to make sense of the Church of England.
I will fill my leisure hours with archaeology and the bass guitar,
With some croquet and even a little archery. So I used to think,
Boasting to myself that I would learn all this,
The move from Ireland to England would suffice.
But what good is talk? I've come all this way
To hear the Buzzcocks sing of boredom
And to waste my best years travelling up and down the A12.
So the metal detector who goes out looking for treasure
Will find, at the end of the day, he has a rucksack stuffed
Not with some Viking hoard, but with a few old cans of 7Up.

50

Let us go, May, let us go. Let us make way for envy,
And flee this Action Short of a Strike,
For here the fudgers and the fixers reign,
And the best lack all conviction.
We could set up our own Hedge School at the Chapel,
Or start a writing consultancy overseas,
Shift camp to Italy, or Tunisia – why not? –
You still have friends over there, don't you?
Shift your arse, my friend, and before
Human Resources terminate our contracts
Let us banish merit with voluntary exile.
How about it? You've heard the story of Ovid:
Exiled over a poem by a blustering emperor,
He settled on the Black Sea and found credit.

54

I've heard you called a waster, but it isn't true,
The fact of the matter is you're a free spirit,
A street philosopher, a thorn in the side of utilitarianism.
If you were eating your brains out to make a killing in the city,
Would you be able to look yourself in the mirror?
The man who has real wealth and knows happiness
Is not the one who busts a gut to please the system
– Crass taught us that – but he who lives for the moment.
So get off your backside, Tackling, and while our employers
Fret over inspections and targets, quality control
And league tables, employability and transferable skills,
Let's go out on the patio and roll a joint,
Before we get another chance we may be dead.
Now is the time for living, and the place is here.

68

I hate the usurious avarice of professors in the Business School,
I hate the Marxist historian's hypocrisy,
I hate the uncommon truthfulness of the lawyer,
And the statistician's secret malice.
I hate the sport scientist just because,
I hate those in Government for rarely keeping their word,
I hate the philosopher for his stupid velvet jacket like Dr Who,
And the lazy specialist in Myth Studies for working so little.
I hate the suave computer scientist, and the boastful set from the International Academy,
Treacherous dramatists, and rhetoricians who talk too much,
Self-important biological scientists, and drunken engineers.
In a word, I hate some vice in every department,
And I hate my own incompetence in online environments,
But above all I hate pedantic administrators.

90

Do not think, White, that these Essex girls,
By hiding their love of self with a winning smile,
Or by hiding their fuck-off faces beneath layers of slap,
Make me forget the girls of Belfast.
The sweetness of the Irish, their lilting speech,
Their neat dress sense, so devoid of show,
It makes me want to throw up when I see these spray-tanned slags.
Eyeing them up when you're clubbing,
You take them all for great beauties,
But when you wake with a sore head
On the filthy mattress that serves them for a bed
Your first thought will be "Who spiced my drink?"
What a nightmare to see how they live …
A young man only has to clap eyes on them to be saved.

95

A thousand curses upon Albert Sloman
For building the University of Essex
And opening the road to Colchester to all,
Bringing permanent congestion to the A12.
Without him students from Spain and France
Would not be bored out of their minds in Essex,
Syrians would not be harassed by immigration
Trapped in a limbo without maintenance or fees,
Undergraduates would not be burdened with debt
Or plagued at weekends by employability workshops,
They would not spend their nights doing shifts at B&Q,
Or plagiarising essays to meet a deadline,
Nor would they find themselves turning to a food bank
At times when they have no money at all.

101

Sheppard, what shall we make of these new Vice-Chancellors,
When we see them all adopting different strategies,
And the least talented rising to the highest honours,
Through vice or virtue, by sheer graft, or without lifting a finger?
One spends cash they don't have and sinks without trace,
Another splashes out and sees recruitment treble,
One makes his mark by acting tough, like a sergeant major,
Another finds that a new Arts Centre gets results.
One makes rapid progress by seeming to dawdle,
Another acts like a slave driver till he comes unstuck,
What's the downfall of one pays dividends for another.
Some assert that the cornerstone of success is knowledge,
Others say that the secret lies in branding alone,
Tell me, Sheppard, which of the two is right?

107

Sometimes, Worpole, I look towards Balkerne Gate,
The Roman wall or the site of the Roman theatre,
Or half a dozen other ancient monuments
Whose remains are scattered within the old town,
And secretly I detest the property developer
Who has buried all this antique beauty
Beneath shopping centres and concrete slabs,
And made a town that is ugly, boring, and uninspired.
Other times I think the town hasn't changed much at all,
There's still a swimming pool, a theatre, even a stadium,
And everywhere you look the faces of squaddies,
Whose power today stretches right up to the university.
Colchester, Worpole, has always been a garrison town,
That's precisely why Boudicca burnt it down.

115

Klein, you don't know how lucky you are
To have escaped this infernal campus when you did,
Before these civil servants of knowledge arrived, with their
      spreadsheets,
Their targets and their Key Performance Indicators.
Where you are, Klein, budget deficits do not hold sway,
Nor do meetings that are constantly proliferating like a Hydra,
Or the unending hatred of an overweight
Administrator, poison your department's core.
With you non-teaching time does not mean idleness,
And nobody works without a pension and holiday pay,
Nor, like the Stasi, do they report on what you say as a joke,
Or freeze your research budgets without notice,
And nobody knows what it is to predict
Annual income and expenditure using Snowball.

stuart mckenzie
the dead weight of beauty

Birch Services M62

Midday weekends I was delivered
to my fate: a fine striped lime green
apron, polyester shirt, navy trousers
too short in the leg, via a mini bus

that went *all round the houses*,
arriving to a *roll call* of cakes
and salads, pot wash and tea point –
told to refuse the *old dears*

who came back to give their bags
another soaking. Health and safety
had my hair tied up in a pony,
while striking miners

tried to trip us as we cleared
away trays and Boy George
sang *"War war is stupid"* on tv
as I fantasized bout painting my lips red.

Earplugs

Some mornings I wake up, find them
pressed into my hair, dangling

like two small clumps of snow
on the ears of a cocker spaniel.

I'd like to ask him upstairs
as he enters his flat,

to please switch off your gristly cough
and mute your feet.

I know silence,
I held it in my hands once:

a one-sided 7" single – so blasphemous
the plant refused to press it.

In place of the song – two minutes of nothing.
I smoothed my fingers across

the empty black grooves,
to the run off – I knew

from beginning to end
would lead nowhere.

Drawing Rosie Huntington-Whiteley's Lips

Your lips have become a signature
I could sign a cheque with – watch

its flimsy paper pout as it pays
for my lunch, plants one

on the cashier then disappears
to the ladies room to touch-up.

I held back from an early break
to work out the science of your

cupids bow, the logistics of being
left handed, its effect on my judgement.

Wrigged up a mechanism
in my mind that would slam

a door shut in my face
to get the pout effect but yours

are pure strawberry whatever that means.
The line of your lips has become

indelible as I'm pushing together
two bits of swollen penne,

now covered in arrabiata on my plate
and they're talking to me, consoling

me – if I should ever shed a tear
over my impending deadline.

A Speck of Glitter

I'm your disco-damaged-darling
distant relative of crushed beetle shell –
a flasher at a beauty spot:
come pitch up a picnic and party.

Not as lavish as malachite,
I'll cling to eyebrows

hitch a lift on cheekbones.
I could never do a day job

or tone it down a notch,
stupidity flickers in me like a light.

I'm two faced – iridescent:
can't trust me to keep my mouth shut.

Action Man

I'm not buying it this time kiddo – you worked
those looks on me once before, I used to

donkey rub your flocked hair and whiskers
across my face, stroke the scar on your cheek

with my thumb as I dressed and undressed you.
Now you jump at the sound of a flick knife –

nothing more than a thrifty shopper closing
the lid of a cracked compact who is gone

before you get the chance to say double crossed –
but hey – you've come over all junk-shop-shy

since I found you naked, tangled up in 3-ply yarn,
nestling with the crochet hooks, knitting patterns –

only a headless He-Man for company. Go on –
gimme one good reason to take you back.

Delinquent

You were never quiet,
neither one to tow the line.
Not quite a queen –
quiff like a sand dune,
your shadow by the dent
of a parked car in a tree lined
street: duet with a fist – a tune
to drop out to – leather clad teen:
do anything for a few quid.

The Dead Weight of Beauty

The last hours were spent cosying up
to the likes of Kate, Linda, Naomi –

the spines of a hundred vintage 80's
– 90's Vogues. His nose now sniffed

at the best parties of bygone eras
sandwiched between Live Aid Chic

and How to Go Boho on a Budget.
His heart was back where it once belonged –

its dull thud petered out below pages
of reportage: a Westwood Retrospective –

super elevated moc croc ghillies that
brought down a Supermodel, bummy skirts,

corsages and corsellettes, bloused and housed
cleavages whispering Vigée Le Brun

Frans Hals and Boucher – a detail
from Daphnis and Chloe: Shepherd

Watching a Sleeping Shepherdess. Now,
his last scene – a Magazine Death Riddle.

Drowned Out by Acid House

The 80s painted us black
and you're still wearing it.
In some bijou backstreet boutique
You ask does the top button fastened
make me look a little
Joy Division ?

Enter Comme des Garçons
with their post Hiroshima chic –
we were all angles back then.
Our nylonness hung from us
like spent umbrellas caught
in the big storm of 1987.

The cigarette burns we endured
to our viscose vêtements –
a kind of frazzled broderie anglaise
caused by fag ends of the niteclub effete elite.
We dressed like the evenings
we try to get through now,

that somehow rendered us
outside of it all:
block printed figures
against an apocalyptic skyline –
before we gave in to high top trainers,
and a sea of mauve tie-dye.

All that Jazz

Bob Fosse got a mention this evening
at your salmon supper I turned down
in place of a take out Veneziana.

Too much coffee – I was all jazz hands
bringing it back: jumping at the sound
of a black sports car's squawking alarm

and the high pitched squeals of punters
hanging out front of the local brasserie.
I love your West End flat and I'm sad

to see you fly off to Japan to teach and
I'm sad at the death of your neighbour too.
Two weeks – to think his body was there

all the time you kept knocking, peering in
through his letterbox. Now, what was it
we were saying about Bob Fosse again?

Bette Davis Impersonator

They know she's his best they've come here to see.
A laughing bag of voices as he glides the stage, one part
whirling dervish, two parts Ninotchka – a Leichner Kabuki.
As homely as a wooden spoon stiring it up – a model T Ford,
a Tin Lizzie seasoned and veteran, a rose petal caught
unfurling beneath a tough shellac sheen – oh, and any colour
so long as its not black. This man beyond his middle age
hiding the sag – the lines beneath the slap, beneath the best
cut that Andre ever did, throwing out the one liners, teutonic
put downs fresh from the make-up bag: words twisted, snarling.
We might be here till Angie Dickinson combs her hair or until
Shelley Winters dies of anorexia. I love it how, chuffing
on a cigarette, he stops, nails it, kills it, delivers to the audience
eyes moving, stalking, as if on cocktail sticks.

After Snow

The blanket's been whipped from us now.
Less than twenty-four hours after its fall
I imagine the fossilled ground releasing
litter – returning to life as limp origami
embossed with trampled smudges of green.

The deadening of the evening's chant:
a slur of words that reached in to us
through an open window – calling
with its cold-muffled sounds, stored,
frozen in its memory, imprinted
with the full feeling of its weight – now gone.

I saw a skeleton scene – a grayscale numbness
through limp fifteen-year-old voile – hung
from 'cafe clips'. Figures stood in monument,
shadows crept out across the park –
packed tight, drooping, slouching with ease:

now small collapsing mounds of presence remain,
its cold is left unfelt and the crisp kiss
of the morning's breeze brings memory, your face.

joey connolly
moderns

THE RIDER'S SONG
Two versions of 'Canción de Jinete', by Federico García Lorca

I.

Córdoba. Apart
        and apart.

Powder-dark horse; charged moon;
unpitted olives loose-panniered and khaki.
A road I believed familiar spells itself out
strangely, uninflected by memory,
                            or Córdoba.

Through dust and across dust
(powder horse; flame moon)
there's a death
        aware and waiting
in the wings and the spires
                of Córdoba.

Ah so long road!
Ah powder-fine horse, stoic and disintegrating!
Ah patient death, that
        skilful interception. Córdoba!

Córdoba! Córdoba.
        Córdoba.

II.

Córdoba: romantic
and apart, and – the *Instituto Cervantes* research grant
blown on olives – lonely as this
bedsit study. I slant my pen to see

an ink-dark horse; an A5 of moon;
unpitted olives loose-panniered and khaki; and,
parting from the river, a road
I considered familiar spelling itself out strangely,
uninflected by memory – *Córdoba*. The word
       is unpocketable as the place.

Through dust and across dust, as
desert and air alternate furiously around
a blinkered horse, a tired-to-bloodshot moon. My eyes,
they weaken. I lose my hands to the sand-laden air,
my thoughts to the pull of *Córdoba*, and my pony,
its becoming its shape, its name. I cannot separate myself.

Ah! Road like a ten-clause-sentence!
Ah! Inky and well-meaning and disintegrating pony!
Ah, my glasses returning to sand, my cash
       to blank discs and paper, and I
all a word loses to its repetition. Córdoba.

  Córdoba.
            Córdoba.

COMING TO PASS
Two versions of a fragment ('Reif Sind, in Feuer getaucht, gehocket...') by Friedrich Hölderlin

    I.

The way fruit, arriving
at its moment of ripeness, is glazed with fire,
cooked and checked by the earth's close process. It's law,
after all, how all things come to pass,
temptress but unearthly. And as
the heavy stake of kindling, resting
on the shoulders, there is much to bear
in mind. But the trails
are evil. And everything
bridled will anyhow
wander off, like horses
into dusk; everything
shot-through with this longing
to go beyond bounds. But so much
stands to be lost. And loyalty
a must; which rules out prophecy
or nostalgia. Let us surrender, be rocked –
cradling ourselves against the moment –
like a boat, lapped by the waves.

II.

For a moment the project
will come perfectly to fruition,
each word glossed by its
plunge into the fire of the present, that flicker
from which everything is once again
made anew. It's almost gospel
the way things arrive, slip askew,
and depart: as a snake,
dreaming of the cloths of heaven, its mounds
of laundry, its drying lines. And as
the weighted intellect, kindle
to any moment's inspiration
or distraction, there is much to bear
in mind. And the previous versions
of the damn thing verge
on the diabolical. And everything
you think you've got bridled, every axiom
you've nailed, will wander off, like horses
into dusk, appearing
to dissolve into the dust of secondary
and tertiary meanings. And the constant
temptation to reach beyond what's
suitable, beyond bounds, into the dense red
of yourself, your vague
and useless gloss. And so much,
so much stands to be lost! And loyalty
a must: this raking up of foreign soil –
the spoiled quarantine of adherence
to original – is no good. No good. All of which
rules out the possibility of prophecy,

or nostalgia. Let us rock between the two,
like a little skin-keeled coracle on a sea of confusion,
lapped by the various camberings
of serial and distinct waves, one
after the other, made up
of the exact same water.

AN OCEAN

Two versions of a fragment ('Antico, sono ubriacato dalla voce...') from Mediterraneo by Eugenio Montale

I.

antique as the best furniture my father
was given to restore, to piece together from other woods;
to fix, and I'm hammered with the voice
that hauls itself from all your mouths, opening
into the moodswing gape of bells, greenish
and self-effacing, ringing into nothingness
and returning. I lived here once, at your shore, the sun
making a midday bakery of every point between these
three horizons, mosquitoes thickening the air. And so I

thicken back into presence, only now
lacking the target-part for the dressing-down
you have for me, the short shrift under your
breath. You showed me
how the petty unrest of my heart
was just a moment's symptom of yours,
your cause; that down at the seafloor of my

life is that incomprehensible absolute:
to be the occurring shift of hugeness, its change and still
to be fixed in place. And so to slough off, like you
the rubble and filth of myself,
the dregs and starfish of your abyss.

II.

ocean is as good a term as any
for the startless thing
you are, and anyhow I'm stripped
of agency, reckless drunk
with a voice which springs from all your mouths –
the bells and pretty lines, the confessions and recollections I can't
keep from getting in,
from soaking what good people have made dry.
I try to find a way the voices
can rise and dissolve into the stuff
they're of. Like waves, but ideas have words
and words ideas and they get
everywhere, sand in sandwiches
at the beach. I think, helplessly, of the place
I used to live; I *Sheffield* and I thicken.
I make recollections like new bread and I absentee myself
from the proper rigours of responsibility. You showed me
the shallows of my heart, how its storming
was only a fractal part of the language
in which it stormed: that down at the seafloor of my life
is that incomprehensible absolute: to be

III.

what Morgan calls *as various as vast,*
yet fixed in place, -- the stability I imagine
of constant renewal, of permanent momentum; the gyroscope
steadied by the movement
of its elements. Galassi
has *voracious* for *vast*, and *fast*
for *various*. And so to work, so
to slough off, like you, the rubble and filth
of myself, the seaweed and the starfish of your abyss.

YOUR ROOM AT MIDNIGHT WAS SUDDENLY
Two versions of 'Ἀπολείπειν ο Θεός Ἀντώνιον' by C. P. Cavaf[

I.

rich with the feeling of your hearing
an unseen procession, a procession rich itself
with the strains of its beauty, a low
darkness of voices – but now
is no time to mourn your loss,
your departing fortune – a life's work
spoiling before your eyes, a host of plans
proving illusory. As if you were
prepared, ever (as if you were brave),
say farewell to the Alexandria that is leaving.

And further: do not allow yourself
the lie of having dreamt, that your ears fail,
or your draining mind. Do not sully this
moment's song with the baseness of your desire
for stability. But as if

you were prepared, ever –
as if you were brave – move,
steady, to the window, as one
given for a city such as this,
this hugeness, move to the window and
beat with the pulse of feeling,
a feeling far off

from the pitched reed and entreaty of cowardice: no,
listen as a fatal delicacy to that voice,
that mass of beauty, that strange
and passing procession off
in the distant absence
of the Alexandria you are anyway losing.

II.

on the table because god knows I'm no
romantic but I
                              want you. And underneath that
we sip our coffee and your eyes
are darker than any history or coffee, than any
Greek coffee ever was and hold the gloss
of immense depth only such darkness has. God knows
I want you to the point
of shucking the woman I love,
our house, the home we built
so slowly. And there is a procession offstage
which accompanies the upward swing
of your eyes, harmonises the argument
for discord, and you're explaining in an
almost unbroken English a poem from the Greek
of Cavafy: I don't know it. As if I were a coward

I keep quiet. On the table of my mind, I mean –
your room – hopeless
coward as I never thought
I was, hopeless neighbour of these
strains of romance language (the names
for your description, the country
my instinct will use to define you), close as I get
to the classicism of your Greek heart,
the close, Doric order of your form.
I don't know what it is which is leaving,
only the sweet draw of its
pain as it goes from me.

THIRD BALLAD
Two versions of 'Ballade III' by Christine de Pizan

I.

And as Leander crossed that salted strait,
alive at his skin to the water, in all its
unsettled electrolytes, all craftless and concealed,
a disappearing small packet of risk, breathing *Hero*
into his fearful shoulder with every
fifth stroke, *Abydos* on the snatched in-breath.
As she waited, Hero, composed of that same, dark water:
>   look how love orders the lover.

Across the sound – from which
so many have shouted – our little Leander pants
for old love, unsatisfactory and noble,
parcelled in the carnation of heat his
chest holds against the near-freezing water.
Against that passage: raw chance, the violence
of numbers, voltage, charts, weather-fronts, a storm.
>   Foresight. See how love orders the lover.

Look how seeing pre-empts the gulf.
And Leander drowned himself in it, noble
and unsatisfactory. And Hero, in all things fit-for-purpose,
lost herself to it, too, at the same time as he,
if later. As this: one cause, one effect.
See this, poor etiolated lovers, at
the seafloor of love's furious cause:
>   look at how love orders the lover. Look

and learn nothing, I *beg* you.
This ordering, this myth-and script-kitty:
we need it, are desperate for it, to overrule our idiot solitude:
look at how love orders the lover.

II.

Always a line I told myself I'd never cross,
this retelling of the Greeks, a long game
I'm utterly without feeling for. And now (no hero, no claim
to heroism) I find you handing me the literal and I folded,
craftless and concealed in the face of
you, your mind, your body. Breathing the metre of it,
Medieval French to English. Parcelling something across.

Look how love orders the lover.

These sounds, these English vowels I've made – if anything –
my home, I shout from them my hectors at the French.
Watch me struggle, craftless in the face of order.
Listen, Frenchy: the gap between our tongues
is just the blackest water, nothingy and unbreathable
with wordlessness, knowable at exactly and only those points
      at which
waves raise like scars from the skin
to catch that scattered, consonantal moonlight.

What survives the crossing? The correspondence
of two white corpses (look how love…)
pushed together by the tide of odds, these
devastated, idiolected lovers. Ten causes,
uncountable effects, a mess of want and
best guess, a sad seafloor of unthinkable love, everybody
just basically wanting to look good,
everybody just trying to write one good poem.
And to push it across, through the nasty insulation

of language, of the straight and the sound.
Don't stop. I'm sorry. Watch
for that washed-up body, whit
and spoken with love.

HISTORY
Two versions of 'ИСТОРИЯ' by Robert Rozhdestvensky

    I.

History! / Picture me, a young man, so / naïve, so deeply
believing / and sincere / over your / absolutes, your palette
of trues. Your / precision of gradient
and angle, / indisputable as a math; / less
questionable / than cliché. / But boys
age, become / grown. Your wind / shades their skin /
and the seconds now / are demanding account
of the centuries. / I write / in the name
of the seconds…

History / has the fructose / beauty of dawn. / History
has the grand / grind of poverty,
structuring people anew / before / scuttling off
in the face of their / degradation. History, /
correct / and senseless. Recall, / now, how frequent
you're called / *appalling*, though / breathtaking, or /
noble though shocking, / shameful, /cruel.
How you depended / on passing / fashion, on ego
and conception: / on dumb façade. How you / shrunk
from the dictators / who measured you by / their own
invented versts and the scrabble / of inches.
Proclaiming your / name, they / stupefied the peoples,
claimed / your protection, and made / worlds, /
lands. You have allowed yourself / to be
powdered, / history, again: rouged and / made up,
again, and redyed, / and again fitted
for a suit of new black. / You were / redrafted / to that
army / of / raucous cries / specialising
in switching / 'great men' / for people:

History! Whore. / *History!* Queen. / You are not
the dust, drying / in archives. History, /
clutch these whispering fingers, / open your
living heart / to the people. / Look, / how
sensibly / your founders, / your
managers and copers / are waking, / are
swallowing their / humble breakfast. / They are hurrying
to kiss their wives, / their goodbyes. The greenery /
of scent covers them, so / excitingly, the high / sun
beats in their eyes, / the horns / flourish their / noise,
and the imperturbable smoke / rises endlessly / from the
        chimneys; /
cries its tired praise against / the still sweep / of skies.
You will, / history, / you will be yet / the most exact
gauge and measure, / the sweet geometry
of pressure. You / will be. You must. It is so / longed-for.

II.

Picture me /see me, a young man /
   hopeless naïf   so deeply
sincere / over your   absolutes /
your palette of   trues
        indisputable as a math / less
questionable than cliché   But boys
    age / your wind shades their skin
  and the seconds now

        I write
      in the name
        of

history   the fructose   beauty of dawn / history
    the grand / grind   of poverty,
  structuring   people /   scuttling off
        degradation
Recall
    you're   *appalling* /
breathtaking
        (mighty / dreadful)

    How you depended   on passing   / on ego
/ on dumb façade.
powdered   again / rouged   / made up

    again / redyed /   and again
fitted for a suit of new black   / redrafted

        raucous cries

whore   queen / you are not the dust
drying in   archives
clutch these   whispering fingers /   open your
       living heart   the people

                  the people

           hurrying
to kiss their   husbands   / the greenery
   of scent

           excitedly   the high   sun
in their   eyes / the horns   their noise

    / the smoke   rises
                              endlessly   cries its
tired praise   / the still   sweep   of skies.
   You will   history   /   you
                                              will

                    the sweet
pressure /   you   will be /   You   must   / it
is

    tomorrow is
          an alternative   to today / a   supplement /
    a   restatement
                        / yesterday

Acknowledgements

Stuart McKenzie

Thanks to the editors of the following publications in which some of these poems have appeared previously: *Envoi, The Interpretor's House, Magma, AnOther Magazine, Urthona*.

Thanks to Maria Trimiklimiotis, Roisin Tierney, Torriano Poetry, Katy Evans-Bush writing group 'The Group' – John Stammers writing group, Lisa Kelly, Sarah Wardle, Jon Sayers and Jet, Daniel Shane, Juan Mateus who have leant me their ears on numerous occasions. Finally to the guy who didn't offer me the job at John Menzies in the Arndale Centre, Middleton, and told me to go to art college – you helped change the course of everything.

Joey Connolly

I'd like to acknowledge the previous translators of these poems, including (but not limited to) Martin Sorrell, Richard Sieburth, Michael Hamburger, Jonathan Galassi, Jamie McKendrick, Edmund Keeley, Philip Sherrard, Maryann Corbett, Nancy Rose, Lyudmila Purgina and – above all and enormously – Edwin Morgan. Edwin Morgan is fantastic. I'd also like to acknowledge the editors of the publications in which some of these poems first appeared: *PN Review, New Poetries VI* (Carcanet), and *Magma*.'